EDUCATION OF ITALIAN RENAISSANCE WOMEN

by

Melinda K. Blade

Revised & Corrected

Mesquite

Ide House

1983

Published by
Ide House, Inc.
4631 Harvey Drive
Mesquite, Texas 75150 U.S.A.

Library of Congress Cataloging in Publication Data

Blade, Melinda K., 1952-
    Education of Italian Renaissance women.

    (Women in history, ISSN 0195-9743 ; no 21b)
    Based on the author's thesis (M.A.T.)–University of
San Diego, 1975.
    Bibliography: p.
    Includes index.
    1. Women--Education--Italy--History. 2. Women--
Italy--History. I. Title. II. Series.
LC2122.B55   1983   376'.945   83-287
ISBN 0-86663-070-8 (lib. bdg.)
ISBN 0-86663-072-4 (pbk.)

In this revised series, this is volume 21b.

For My Parents

Desiderius Erasmus of Rotterdam (1466?-1536)
Celebrated classical scholar and Christian humanist, as engraved by
Albrecht Durer (1526)

EDITOR'S PREFACE

Sixteenth century Renaissance history has fascinated humankind since its epoch age. Melinda K. Blade has presented in this essay one of its most interesting—and little studied—facets.

Much of the growth of modern educational philosophy began in this unique time. Much of this growth was generated by one extraordinary universal man: Desiderius Erasmus (c. 1466-1536), who is often considered the link between humanism of the south and humanism of the north—and the mainstay of education for all western civilized individuals. Like Petrarch in the fourteenth century (and Voltaire in the eighteenth century) Erasmus dominated his world and its intellectual life, giving inspiration and courage to many who would come after him. His own knowledge was remarkable: educated as a child by the Brethren of the Common Life, he later went to Venice and Padua to improve his Greek, commenting "For without Greek, Latin is shallow rivulets. Greek is the stream truly running with gold."

So expert did he become in Greek, having studied under the Cretan Marcus Musurus, that he published Latin translations of several plays by Euripides, and of the satirist Lucian. His expert handling of the Greek tongue so enthused and excited his contemporaries that they too raced to learn this ancient and beautiful language. To spirit on this particular form of learning even further, Erasmus penned the famous *Adages* which became the most widely read book (after the Bible) in the sixteenth century.

From the *Adages*, Erasmus proceed to publish the first printed edition of the Greek New Testament—based on only a relatively few manuscripts which were available. Although his edition is inferior to that of Jimènez de Cisneros of Àlcala, it had an even greater influence—quickening nobles throughout Europe to set up special schools to teach the ancient languages—schools in which they would place their sons and daughters in hopes that by studying the ancient

England found its most talented humanist and educator in Sir Thomas More (1478-1535), who was a close friend of Desiderius Erasmus of Rotterdam, and Lord Chancellor under King Henry VIII (reigned 1509-1547). A devout Roman Catholic, he espoused Christian humanism in his prolific writings, the best known one being *Utopia* (Greek for nowhere). He won great favor with the king when he stood out against Martin Luther, and possibly helped Henry author his treatise *Assertio Septem Sacramentorum*, for which the king was given the title *Fidei Defensor*, but Sir Thomas fell from royal favor when Henry wished to rid himself of his first wife Catherine of Aragon on the grounds, the king argued, that he had married within the prohibited degrees of canon law. More was executed, by being beheaded when he would not support the king's petition for a writ of divorce.

sidered essential to any rounded education, and thus made mandatory for both sexes). Vittorino was a difficult task-master, requiring all of his students to excel or give up exhausted. Most succeeded, and those who did went on to significant positions within church and state. Miss Blade has especially captured the impact of the d'Este sisters. This is also true in her presentation of the role of Vives in the education of renaissance women. Born in Valencia, Juan Luis Vives (d. 1540) received a traditional education, but imbibed humanist ideas in his youth which led him to France to study at the University in Paris, and later at the Louvain where he wrote a sterling commentary on Saint Augustine's *City of God* which won him the approval of Erasmus and More. Although he spent most of his time at Bruges, because of his correspondence and friendship with both More and Erasmus, Vives frequently traveled to England where he enjoyed the favor of Queen Catherine who prayed he stay to tutor her daughter Mary.

The education of Mary Tudor was classic, and if it had not been for the marital affairs and concerns of Henry VIII, Vives might have remained in England. However, when the king sought to get rid of his "barren" wife, Vives came to the open support of Catherine which forced him finally to leave the kingdom and return to Bruges. He continued to corresponde with More and Erasmus until More was sent to his death by the king; he continued to correspond with Erasmus until death separated the two.

From Erasmus Vives became deeply interested and impressed with the moral aspects of humanism. To this end he wrote a number of treatises which raised his name to being equal to "a second Quintilian." His *Causes of the Corruptions of the Arts* discusses the problem of study and criticizes the conventional methods of education. Like Vittorino da Feltre, Vives believed that Greek and Latin should be taught, but argued that the mother tongue should not be neglected: he regarded the skillful use of the native idiom to be not only a necessary tool in direct communication with peers and laborers, but also a sign of a truly educated human being. Religion was to be taught, and boys and girls alike were to be drilled in grammar, syntax, and rhetoric.

languages their children would become morally sound and spiritually alive. There was one school which predated these new institutions. Established by Gian Francesco I (d. 1444), it administered a rigid scholastic program which allowed only men to study the smattering of learning available at that time. However this improved when Giovanni Francesco Gonzaga (1466-1519) invited Vittorino da Feltre to bring into the curriculum the new humanism.

Education to da Feltre meant a detailed and developed form of critical classicism. Nearly single-handedly da Feltre revived classical education at Mantua—and with it gave new meaning to the term classical education, for traditional methods of learning were considered too banal and too practical to be truly educative and enlightening. Da Feltre sought to raise ideals and interests along with thought in general and particular above the mundane day-to-day problems surrounding the men and women of his day. To do this he built upon the contributions of Vergerio (*De Ingenuis Moribus*, or *On Good Manners*: a first book of popular ettiquette), so that the individual would become fully rounded to fit comfortably within any situation or level of society. To complete this goal da Feltre argued that women needed an education, too—and ought best to be taught along side with men—but without any special benefits due their sex. It was his belief that if the sexes were taught together they would mutually help the other to higher levels of refinement and personal advancement, attain greater piety, and willingly become prepared to assume social responsibilities—regardless if those responsibilities were placed upon them by their teacher, family, state, or church.

To be prepared for all things, da Feltre argued, humankind needed to have more than a mere vocational education. It would not always be necessary to know mathematics—for bankers may become too numerous, as would be the case for merchants and others involved with figures; the same was true for military sciences, or any other vocational learning. Instead, da Feltre argued, it was imperative that all people acquire a classical education, learning Greek and Latin, literature, music, and the fine arts (especially drawing), along with a sensible physical education which would include horseback riding, fencing, swimming, and marching (which was con-

Vives was quite modern in one regard. Like Erasmus, Juan Luis Vives did not believe that the end of formal education came with the amassing of mere erudition, but rather continued on as demonstrated by the acquisition of knowledge which would make possible better living. This is the final thesis of the Blade contribution.

—Arthur Frederick Ide
Eastfield College

Feast of St. Michael the Archangel
1982

The extent of how far women were educated—and how
men both recognized and feared an educated woman—
is seen in the sixteenth century woodcut illustration of
the Protestant Scot reformer John Knox (1505-1572)
who blasted his trumpet of reform in the ears of Mary,
Queen of Scots (reigned 1542-1567, beheaded in
1587) who was known as one of the most literate
women of her day. The text accompanying the carac-
ture reads, "No Queen in her kingdom can or ought to
sit fast, if Knox's. . .books blow any true blast."
Knox's argument was that in educating a woman a man
lessened his own dignity and defied the will of God,
citing the Pauline condemnation of women speaking in
religious ceremonies, requiring women to turn to
their husbands for all needs and information. Mary,
Queen of Scots, had little patience for Knox.

INTRODUCTION

To place the educational advances of Italian Renaissance women in perspective, it is prudent to consider, among other factors, the limited amount of education that was available to medieval women. In addition, a reflective glance at the turbulent conditions which existed in Europe toward the end of the Middle Ages reveal their relationship to the educational advances made by Italian Renaissance women.

In regard to the type of education that was available to medieval women, it must be noted that there is a scarcity of recorded literature about the subject.* In this regard, Mary Beard (1876-1958)[1] expressed the opinion that the lack of recorded matter primarily exists because historians have neglected women. In fact, Mrs. Beard believed that historians' emphasis on publicizing men makes it appear that only men make history worthy of recording—an opinion shared by other writers.[2] Such stress by historians on masculine achievements led Mrs. Beard to remark in regard to the education of medieval women, ". . . It is difficult to see the tree of women's education in the forest of controversial and masculine literature."[3]

After taking historians to task for their neglect of medieval women and women's role in history, Mrs. Beard further commented that it is a misconception to believe that the education of medieval women is of little consequence in the development of western civilization. She contended that recorded literature by students of the Middle Ages exists which referred to women in convents as being educated "by some process."[4] Furthermore, Mrs. Beard asserted that medieval women conducted schools to train nuns and to educate girls of the upper social strata.[5] She noted, however, that historians have given minimal consideration to the effect that educated women of medieval times had an history.

Mary Beard acknowledged that it is easy to find many references to the inferiority of medieval women of the period, but she declared in a strong voice that one can also find references by many Catholic historians and teachers who refute that point.[6] For example, Mrs. Beard referred to Dominican mystics teaching girls and to Pierre DuBois' (1250-1312) belief that since the Ifidel had not been conquered by violence, "girls should be taught theology and medicine to overcome the Infidel by the swords of the spirit and service."[7] Thus, DuBois' statement makes it fair to infer that although a limited education was available to medieval women, he believed that medieval girls possessed the intellect needed to understand both theology and medicine.

To bolster her arguments concerning the role of medieval women in regard to education and history, Mrs. Beard contended that existing records reveal that lower and upper class medieval women were educated in some manner and had a variety of intellectual interests. She mentioned that reading, writing, debating current issues, and corresponding with other women were some of the feminine intellectual pursuits of that era. Mrs. Beard also stated that medieval women frequently corresponded with male scholars and that women who were associated with the mystics did "voluminous writing."[8] Thus, it appears that the women of the Middle Ages were educated, albeit in a limited manner.

In a further attempt to place the education of Italian Renaissance women in its proper perspective, it should be noted that the late fourteenth century was a time of upheaval and anxiety throughout Europe. The Hundred Year's War (1337-1453) raged between France and England, while the Black Death (1348-1349) left famine, pestilence and death in its wake. The papacy was evicted from its centuries-old base in Rome, to a new headquarters in the City of Avignon, and the Church's eventual split into two rival factions led to the Schism of the Church in 1378 to 1417. In the midst of these trends, various members of different social groups lost confidence in the doctrine and institutions

Above: **The Palace of the Popes, Avignon.** This enormous fortresslike palace was constructed during the "Babylonian Captivity" of the papacy (1334-1352) to ward off disease, outside influence, and keep the landless and disheartened away. Below: **Woodcut of Rome**, from Sebastian Munster's *Cosmographiae* (1544), shows the original St. Peter's (upper-right), with the Pantheon dome in the center [from the Bildarchiv d. Ost. Nationalbibliothek, Vienna]

Palazzo Strozzi, Florence; construction begun in 1484 by one of the richest merchant families in Italy, this palace is a superb example of Florentine use of rusticated stone blocks and heavy cornices, producing a massively imposing and sturdy, but balanced facade, being able to withstand popular uprisings, invasions and war, and the passage of time. *Courtesy of the Italian Government Travel Office.*

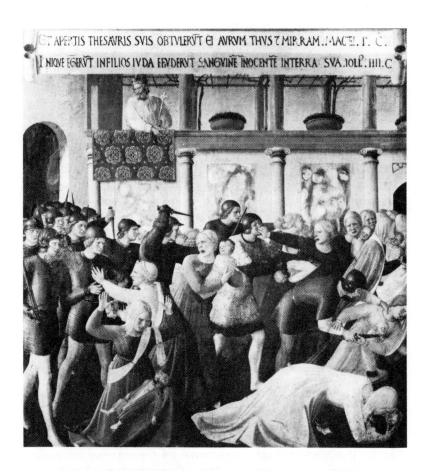

Massacre of the Innocents by Fra Angelico. This paint-
ing was commissioned by Piero de Medici as a part of a
series on the life of Christ. Although the theme is
based on the story of King Herod's men executing all
male infants at the time of the birth of Christ, contemporary violence in fifteenth-century Italy certainly may
have influenced the artist-monk—a man of vision and
ability who composed the scene with great delicacy
coupled with an extraordinary realism as can be seen
in the swaddling of the infants, design of the tapestry,
and braids of the women. *Alinari/Editorial Photocolor
Archives.*

of the Church.[9] Additionally, the teachings in the universities became narrow in scope and rigid in context as the
Church desperately sought to restore some semblance of
order to a changing world.[10]

As a reaction against the prevailing trends, the humanists, a new breed of scholar and philosopher, emerged—within
and without—the Church. The humanist felt that the classical Greek, Roman, and original Christian ideals had been lost
amidst the chaotic turmoil of medieval Europe. For that
reason, it was the basic purpose of the humanist to return to
the ideas of the distant past. As an antiquarian, he advocated
the study of Latin, Hebrew and Greek languages, while plac-
ing emphasis on education, poetry, history, the nature of
man, and natural phenomena. He believed that such a curriculum would result in renewed life and hope amidst the
despair that permeated Europe during the late Middle Ages.

Despite the humanist's optimism, the social and political
conditions that existed in Italy during the early Renaissance
period seemed unfavorable to the advancement of intellectual
interests. The duchies and the kingdoms were beset by
foreign invasions and local wars. The prince and the *condot-
terie*[11] were either in the field waging war or were on the
defensive. Party discontent in the various republics led to
family feuds which served to threaten individuals and individual freedom.[12]

The political games of chance caused the fortunes of
leaders to vacillate. While the leader's fortunes were fluctu-
ating, the merchant class benefitted by the state of increasing
commercial activity and by domestic patronage. As a result,
the merchant class rose to a position of wealth and security.
Thus, amid the scenes of civic festivities and military
triumphs, the rebirth of learning came into being. Strangely,
there were no indicators of conflict between the apparent
desire for power and avarice for gain and the contradictory
desire for the intellectual riches of the ancients.

From the onset, the nobles and the merchant princes
encouraged the leaders of the movement to revive classical
learning. The nobility and the merchant class placed gener-
ously ample portions of their profits at the disposal of the
authors of the movement.[13] Libraries were founded to
receive the revered manuscripts and schools were started.[14]

Procession of Flagellants. The grimness of the Black Death provoked excesses among the living who believed that the disease was God's punishment for the sins of humanity. Above depicts a procession of robed and hooded flagellants with two of their men flogging those ahead of them (*Bibliotheque Royale Albert I, Brussels);* below (*Walters Art Gallery*) The Plague Stricken showing the extent of the Death where a man collapses with the symptomatic buba on his neck, while St. Sebastian pleads for mercy as a winged devil attacks an angel.

16

**The Three Living and the
Three Dead, c. 1345**
*These pages from the psal-
ter and prayer book of the
Bonne of Luxembourg re-
veal the fascination with
sudden death that per-
vaded much of the popular
art of the fourteenth century.*   The Metropolitan
Museum of Art. The Clois-
ters Collection 1969

Death makes him tremble, turn pale,
His nose curves, his veins swell,
His neck bursts, his flesh melts,
His joints and tendons grow and swell,
Feminine body, who are so tender,
Smooth, soft, and so precious;
Must all these evils await thee?
Yes, or you must go to heaven alive.

These wealthy patrons were individuals who warmly embraced the Renaissance, seeking to make the Renaissance wealth their own.[15]

As the leaders of society's acceptance of the Renaissance increased, the humanist movement mushroomed, spreading from scholars, philosophers, and poets, to artists and architects. Indeed, the movement served as the spiritual focal point of the Renaissance.

By the middle of the sixteenth century, a network of humanist artists and scholars permeated Europe. As a result of this wide-spread movement, women, who had long been considered man's inferior,[16] benefitted: since the humanists stressed the value of education believing that it led to virtue, the humanist felt that the more knowledgeable a person was, the more virtuous the person. Consequently, the education of Renaissance women, as well as men, was of equal importance to the humanist and for the first time in western history, emphasis was now placed on educating females.

Although humanist ideals led many scholars, writers and philosophers to accept the concept of education for women, there were many men who were opposed to changing the medieval concept of women's position of inferiority to men. Although educator's opinions varied concerning the prudence of educating women, H. J. Mozans (1851-1921) stated that during the Renaissance "...the remarkable flowering of the intellect of the Italian women was seen at its best."[17] Will Durant (1885-1982) reinforced Mozans' opinion by commenting that "the emergence of women was one of the brightest phases in that period."[18] It is this "bright phase" or opportunity and new view on the value of education and the educability of women, which spurred many women to emerge from the cloistered, dark recesses of the past.

NOTES

[*The Education of Medieval Women (vol. 110 in the Ide House series Woman in history will be published in 1983.) fills this need.]

[1] Mary R. Beard, Women as Force in History (3d ed.; New York: Collier Books, 1973), p. 255; see chap. 3 for assessment of the neglect

of women. For a critique of this book see Bernice A. Carroll's "Mary Beard's *Women as Force in History*: A Critique," in *Women: An Issue*, ed. Lisa Baskin, Lee R. Edwards and Mary Heath (Boston: Little, Brown and Co., 1972), pp. 125-143. For a contemporary appraisal see *La Querelle des Femmes* including *Cyte of Ladyes* by Christine de Pisan, and Erasmus of Rotterdam's *Christiani matrimonii institutio* (Basel, 1526), chap. 17.

[2]Beard, *ibid.*, Cf. Simone de Beauvoir, *The Second Sex*, trans. H. M. Parshley (New York: Bantam Books, 1961), pp. xix-xx.

[3]Beard, *loc. cit.*.

[4]*Ibid.;* cf. Lena Eckstein, *Women Under Monasticism* (Cambridge [Eng.]: Cambridge University Press, 1896), pp. 479-480 for a commentary on the studies pursued in medieval convents.

[5]*Upper strata*, here, refers to the patrician and merchant class. Cf. Cornelius Heinrich Agrippa, *De nobilitate et praecellentia foeminei sexus declamatio* (Paris, 1713), pp. 17-18ff.

[6]One reference concerning the inferiority of medieval women is Eileen Powers "The Position of Women," in *The Legacy of the Middle Ages*, edited by C. G. Crump and E. F. Jacob (New York: Oxford University Press, 1926), pp. 403-433.

[7]Beard, *op. cit.*, p. 256. Cf. Christopher Hare [Mrs. Marion Andrews], *The Most Illustrious Ladies of the Renaissance* (London: Harper and Brothers, 1911), p. 38. Cp. Louise Labe (c. 1520-1566) in *Les poetes lyonnais precurseurs de la Pleiade*, edited by J. Aynard (Paris, 1924), pp. 157-159.

[8]Beard, *ibid.*, p. 257. For other sources concerning the education of medieval women, see especially Frederick Eby and Charles F. Arrowood, *The History of Philosophy and Education: Ancient and Medieval* (Englewood Cliffs, N.J.: Prentice-Hall, 1940); and, *Education Charters and Documents*, edited by A. F. Leach (New York: Cambridge University Press, 1911); additional bibliography is found at the end of this book.

[9]For a detailed study of the papacy see H. B. Cotterill, *Italy from Dante to Tasso: 1300-1600* (New York: Frederick A. Stokes Co., 1919), pp. 203-227. Cf. J. H. Plumb, *The Italian Renaissance* (New York: Harper Torchbooks, 1961), pp. 79-94.

[10]For additional information concerning the medieval university, see Iris Wilson Engstrand, "Student Life in the Medieval University," *History Journal* I (Spring, 1975), pp. 53-62; F. M. Powicke, "Some Problems in the History of the Mediaeval University," in *Transactions*

of the Royal Historical Society, 4th ser., XVII (London), p. 4; Robert F. Seybolt, *The* Manuale Scholarium*: An Original Account of Life in the Mediaeval University* (Cambridge, Mass.: Harvard University Press, 1921), p. iii; Astrik L. Gabriel, "The Ideal Master of the Mediaeval University," *The Catholic Historical Review* LX (April, 1974), pp. 1-40. For an excellent assessment of the problems faced by the Church, see Roland H. Bainton, *Christendom* (2 vols.; New York: Harper Torchbooks, 1966) I, pp. 224-254. Cf. Brian Tierney, *The Crisis of Church and State: 1050-1300* (Englewood Cliffs, N.J.: Prentice-Hall, 1964), pp. 165-210.

[11]The *condottiere* were the military leaders of mercenary armies in Renaissance Italy. For information concerning the significance of the *condottiere* see *The History of Nations*, Henry Cabot Lodge, editor of the 6th ed., vol. 4: *Italy* (New York: P.F. Collier and Son, Ltd., 1928), pp. 251-256. A contemporary picture is in Niccolo Machiavelli, *History of Florence and the Affairs of Italy*.

[12]J.C.L. Sismondi, *History of the Italian Republics in the Middle Ages*, edited by William Boulting (London: George Routledge and Sons, Ltd., 1895) Bk. II, which provides the background of the Guelph and Ghibelline feud. See also Lodge, *loc. cit.*, chaps. 29 and 30; and, Ferdinand Schevill, *The Medici* (2d ed.; New York: Harper Torchbooks, 1960), pp. 15ff.

[13]The de Medicis were one of the most generous of patrons to humanist authors; see Schevill, *op. cit.*, for an assessment of the Medici role in the revival of the arts. J. H. Plumb, *loc. cit.*, pp. 51-56, also discusses the Medici contribution. Cf. E. L. S. Harsburgh, *Lorenzo the Magnificent and Florence in Her Golden Age* (London: n.p., 1909).

[14]The popes were among the most avid collectors of manuscripts; see Plumb, *op. cit.*, pp. 84-85; Lodge, *op. cit.*, pp. 296-300; cf. Schevill, *op. cit*, pp. 183-212 for an assessment of the Medici popes' contributions to the arts.

[15]Jacob Burkhardt, *The Civilization of the Renaissance in Italy*, trans. by S.C.C. Middlemore (2d ed.; London: The Phaidon Press, 1944). Emil Lucki, *History of the Renaissance* (5 vols.; Salt Lake City, Utah: University of Utah Press, 1963). Lewis W. Spitz, *The Renaissance and Reformation Movements* (2 vols.; Chicago: Rand McNally, 1972).

[16]See Chap. One, below; cp. John Addington Symonds, *The Renaissance in Italy* (7 vols.; London: Smith, Elder, and Co., 1897).

[17]H. J. Mozans [J. A. Zahms], *Women in Science* (New York: D. Appleton & Co., 1913), p. 57.

[18]Will Durant, *The Story of Civilization*, vol. 5: *The Renaissance* (New York: Simon and Schuster, 1953), p. 581.

The Print Shop. A detail of a sixteenth century printing establishment, showing the development of the division of labor: the setting of type, inking the chase, operating the press, and drying the leaves of paper once printed. The growth of printing enabled women in Italy and throughout Europe to read and grow faster intellectually. A limited number of women even entered the printing profession—and in some cases successfully challenged men as quality craftsmen in the art of printing. (Photo: Radio Times Hulton Picture Library.)

THE CUMAEAN SIBYL
CEILING, SISTINE CHAPEL. VATICAN. ROME

MICHELANGELO. 1475—1564

CHAPTER ONE

Educational and Social Conditions During the Renaissance

The emergence of Italian Renaissance women and the flowering of the intellect of Italian Renaissance women was not without a struggle: men dominated women in most areas. For example, in times of war, men were the warriors and the only place for Renaissance women during the campaign was as camp followers. In the political arena, with few exceptions, men dominated: their role was that of the head of the state and where there was any semblance of democracy, men served as the legislators. In the field of skilled labor, men dominated also: their role was that of head of their households and the provider. He toiled in craft guilds, on farms, at the forge, and in semi-skilled positions. The woman was kept occupied at home. Likewise, in the realm of goods production, women were equally restricted. Peasant women worked only in the home, in the fields, or as domestics while upper-strata women were excluded from the areas of goods production. Some modern-day writers stress the fact that women have been "oppressed . . . throughout history."[1] In relationship to the Renaissance attitude toward the status of women, Mozans remarked that the male sex assumed superiority over the female, since women were "but an accident, an imperfection, an error of nature."[2] Moreover, Mozans stressed that Renaissance women were man's property, and as such were meant to serve either as a servant attending man's comforts or to provide him pleasure or entertainment: dancing, usually partnered by another female, and solo singing to the accompaniment of a lute, being the most popular form of entertainment. Topical subjects were frequently debated. Furthermore it should be noted that women were considered to be *"masoccasionaties—*a man marred in the making".[3]

Marzieh Gail (fl. 1960) further strengthened the evidence concerning man's superiority to women of early times by stating that during the Renaissance "the birth of a girl was no cause for rejoicing."[4] Mary Beard commented that from the bulky writings of early and late clerics, passages emphasizing the lowly status of women can be found. Clerical works reveal that women were not only considered to be inferior, they were also considered to be dangerous. The records contain passages suggesting that women should be suppressed and that the door of learning should forever be closed to them. Mrs. Beard noted,[5] however, that passages can be found in the cleric's works which show that women's inferiority to man was not a universal theory held by the Church.

Chronicles of the Renaissance support the fact that women have paralleled the literary taste and accomplishments of leading men of the same era. In fact, some historians of the Renaissance argue that Italian women played a significant role in the rebirth and restoration of classical learning.[6] The history of Italian literature indicates that many women were skilled in Latin and Greek, not only speaking those languages with ease, but also writing both prose and poetry in these classical tongues. They did not neglect cultivation of their native tongue, since the vernacular was used in correspondence with relatives and friends. The seed of culture was also evident by its usage in their writings of sonnets and hymns.[7]

How then did Italian women come to enjoy educational advantages that were not shared by other European women? Mozans believed that women in other European areas, particularly in England and Germany, were feeling the adverse effects that resulted from the suppression of the convents which had been destroyed by the Reformers. Since the convents had been the mainstay of education for centuries, the affected areas stagnated educationally while Italy's educational movement progressed.[8]

In addition to the suppression of the convents, other factors were involved which led Italy's Renaissance movement to emerge before the rebirth of education in other European areas. During the Renaissance, Italy was the natural hub of activity, primarily as the seat of the Church was in Rome. The geographical proximity of many people to the

ALBRECHT DURER: THE FOUR HORSEMEN OF THE APOCALYPSE.
From right to left, representatives of war, strife, famine, and
death gallop across Christian society leaving thousands dead or
in misery. The horrors of the age made this subject extremely
popular in art, literature, and sermons. (Courtesy, Museum
of Fine Arts, Boston)

papacy enabled them to see that the papacy was engaged in political affairs. This involvement was thought of as a contradiction of the spirit of the papacy, whose spiritual supremacy included all nations. Some patricians held that the papacy's days as a great spiritual authority no longer existed, and thus they ceased to respect the papacy to the same degree which Christians did in other areas. Furthermore, prominent humanistic Italians believed that the majority of the revenues which were coming to the Church from all parts of Europe were being used in two ways: to increase the papal possessions, or to promote small local wars. These humanists argued that the Church was strictly a business organization and thus they became skeptical about the infallibility of the Church and the pope's authority.[9] These reasons, combined with other factors, gave rebirth to education and the cultivation of the arts in Italy at an earlier date than elsewhere in Europe.

Although some Italian women gained knowledge of learning prior to their European counterparts, it should be noted that many historians agree that only a select group of Italian women enjoyed educational advantages during the Renaissance and thereafter.[10] Only those women who could claim nobility by reason of birth or those who were wives or daughters of scholars, enjoyed the fruits of education. According to Mozans, women who failed to fall into those specific categories "remained in the state of complete illiteracy."[11] To emphasize his point, Mozans declared that Renaissance women other than those in the upper social strata were relegated, "according to a Breton saying, to look after altar, hearth and children—*La femme se doit garder l'autel, le feu, les enfants.*"[12] In that vein, Durant reinforced Mozans by stating that lower class females were destined to "carry domestic burdens and family headaches to their graves."[13]

NOTES

[1]Bernice A. Carroll, "Mary Beard's *Women as Force*", p. 132. Cf. Gerda Lerner, "The Feminists: A Second Look," *Columbia Forum* 13 (Fall, 1970), p. 26. A similar view of male domination in political, economic, and cultural areas is expressed in "Redstockings Manifesto,"

Sisterhood is Powerful, ed. Robin Morgan (New York: Vintage Books, 1970), p. 534; cf. Matilda J. Gage, *Women, Church and State* (New York: The Truth Seekers Co., 1893).

[2]Mozans, *op. cit.*, p. 2.

[3]*Ibid.*; cf. Marzieh Gail, *Life in the Renaissance* (New York: Random House, 1968), p. 40.

[4]*Ibid.*.

[5]Beard, *op. cit.*, p. 256.

[6]Mozans, *op. cit.*, p. 58.

[7]A general treatment of the topic is Maud F. Jerrold, *Vittoria Colonna: With Some Account of Her Friends and Her Times* (New York: Books for Libraries Press, 1969); see also, Julia Cartwright, *Isabella d'Este, Marchioness of Mantua, 1474-1539: A Study of the Renaissance* (2 vols; New York: E.P. Dutton and Co., 1903), and her *Beatrice d'Este, Duchess of Milan, 1475-1497: A Study of the Renaissance* (London: J.M. Dent and Sons, Ltd., 1912).

[8]Mozans, *op. cit.*, pp. 55-56; cf. *ibid.*, p. 75, quoting Thomas Fuller, chaplain to Charles II, as it appeared in *Church History* 3 (1845) p. 336.

[9]Cf. Marsiglio of Padua, "Defensor Paci," in *Marsilius of Padua*, ed. by Alan Gewirth (2 vols; New York: Columbia University Press, 1951, 1956); Niccolo Machiavelli, *The Prince and The Discourses* (New York: Modern Library, 1940); Martin Luther, "95 Theses", in *Documents Illustrative of the Continental Reformation*, ed. Beresford James Kidd (Oxford: Clarendon Press, 1911), doc. 11. For the full flavor of the argument it is most graphic in the pounding argument of Martin Luther in his "Address to the German Nation" (the best edition is *An den Christlichen Adel Deutscher Nation*: Halle: Berein für Reformationsgeschichte, 1884). The Italian equivalent is from the pen of Savanarola: see *Girolamo Savanarola*, ed. Roberto Ridolfi (2 vols.; Florence: n.p., 1952), vol. 1, chap. 1, pp. 193ff., and vol. 2, pp. 15, 184, 230. Cf. G. A. Capponi, *Storia della Republica di Firenze* (2 vols.; Florence, n.p., 1875).

[10]This viewpoint is opposed by Mary Beard, who argued: "...Linguistic and literary development was not confined to the ruling circles. ...Classical schools for girls and boys were opened in Italian cities, giving to the business and professional circles, as well as to patricians, opportunities to acquire knowledge of the ancient languages and the natural or secular philosophies embodied in Greek and Latin literature." Beard, *op. cit.*, p. 262,

[11] Mozans, *op. cit.*, p. 71.

[12] *Ibid.*, p. 74.

[13] Durant, *op. cit.*, p. 582.

**Peasants Dancing, by Albrecht Dürer
(1471–1528)**
German Information Center photo

CHAPTER TWO

The Education of Italian Women During the Renaissance

Historians are in general agreement on the main aspects of education of youth of the Renaissance. It is a generally accepted fact that in comparison to the limited education available to medieval women, upper strata Italian Renaissance women and girls received broad educations, basically equivalent to that experienced and enjoyed by Renaissance men and boys. In fact, Mozans stated[1] unequivocally that upper class women enjoyed equal scholastic freedom with their male counterparts. Durant concurred[2] by declaring that under the guidance of tutors or nuns, the daughters of upper class parents received an education comparable to that of the average man of her social status.

In a further example of male-female scholastic equality among the upper class youths, Jacob Burkhardt (1818-1897) observed that the Italian humanist had no aversion to having his sons and daughters equally participate in the same philological or literary courses. In fact, he was glad the opportunity was available to his daughters.[3]

In addition to agreeing that both boys and girls of the period under discussion received relatively equal educations, historians are in general accord regarding lower class girls being educated in their homes. Since their mothers were their sole tutors lower class girls' educations were understandably limited and destined the girls to perform domestic duties, especially caring for their children.

Although the mothers of both upper and lower class girls played some part in their daughters' educations, the fathers played no role at all. However, then, as is frequently the case now, the upper class fathers paid the cost of the tutors for their daughters.

Portrait of a Young Lady, 1569
British School   XVI Century
Tate Gallery (T.400)

Even though they had an academic advantage over women of earlier periods, the girls of well-to-do Renaissance families were relatively secluded in their homes or convents until they reached a marriageable age.[4] It was not uncommon for six year old girls to be skilled in household arts and sewing since upper strata girls were raised to efficiently manage their future homes and servants.

All girls learned to brew herbs for medicinal use, bind fractured limbs, nurse fevers and colds, and to perform simple medical practices. It is reasonable to assume that this general knowledge of medicine led some Renaissance women to enter the medical field. For example, Dorotea Bucca (1400-1436) occupied a chair of medicine at the University of Bologna, lecturing with distinction, on full par with her male counterpart at the University, and others elsewhere.[5]

Although acquiring such useful talents, it was the accepted custom for young women of this period to serve a basic apprenticeship learning the social graces. Young women were primarily educated in the social graces, since charm, chastity, modesty, reserve, and composure were highly stressed. Virtue in Renaissance women was the Italian ideal. For those reasons, the social graces of dancing, singing, and playing such musical instruments as the zithern, harp, and the lute were considered to be a basic part of the girls' education. Likewise, cooking skills, etiquette, and effective use of cosmetics, and the art of flirting prior to seeking a husband, were highly touted during the so-called apprenticeship.[6] In regard to the quest of many Renaissance girls for husbands, even the personal reading habits of the young women reflected, in part, that goal, as their reading served a two-fold purpose:[7]

> First, a personal aethetic aim, the reinvigoration and refreshment of their souls; secondly an aim relating to their apostolic mission, the art of understanding men's souls, then charming and leading them by means of conversation.

Basic literary selections of the girls included literature by Dante (1265-1321), Virgil (70-19 B.C.), Petrarch (1304-1374), and Horace (65-8 B.C.). For lighter reading, they chose current romantic tales, especially the ribald works of Giovanni Boccaccio (1313-1375). Boccaccio wrote bawdy

32

MADONNA, CHILD AND ANGELS
NATIONAL GALLERY, LONDON

MICHELANGELO. 1475—1564

*Michaelangelo's recognition of the growing importance
in educating women can be seen by the testimony of
the book in the Madonna's hand.*

tales of medieval France and Italy, and his famous *Deca-meron* gave a matter-of-fact view of human fraility. Of such earthy works as Boccaccio's, Ludovico Dolce (1508-1568),[8] and Juan Luis Vives[9] cautioned young women to avoid them. In fact, Vives denounced such literature by declaring that "I would rather see a girl deaf and blind than thus overstimulated to pleasure. . . ."[10]

Still historians' views differ concerning some aspect of Renaissance education. William Woodward (1874-1950) contended[11] that the humanist[12] contemplated an equal range of subjects and standards of achievement for both Italian Renaissance boys and girls. Woodward pointed out, however, that the humanist, while educating girls, was not attempting to change the status of women: the humanist might offer the girls the same educational subject matter as boys, but Woodward like Mozans,[13] and Durant,[14] felt that women's primary duties were "home, social life, the rearing of children, the practice of charity and religious obligations."[15] Furthermore, Woodward injected what he labeled the element of "intellectual distinction."[16] The label emerged from the humanist's philosophy that woman's first care should be a well-ordered life and practice of religion. To help girls attain this goal, the humanist presented educational subjects to girls which emphasized those aspects of her training. In contrast, according to the Renaissance educator Vittorino da Feltre,[17] the education of boys was aimed at the "development of the complete citizen."[18] Likewise, Pietro Paolo Vergerius (1498-1565), the Italian educator, believed[19] that the ideal of the male's education was in "the perfection of man as Citizen."

Although the goals differed, the education of upper class Renaissance youth dealt with similar subjects—literature, history, astrology, and others. In Latin literature, girls primarily read Augustine of Hippo's *Confessions* and *City of God*, and Lactantius (c. 250-330), since they were recognized not only as stylists, but also as sound theologians. In addition to Latin literature, the girls' studies also included such writers as Cicero and Seneca (3 B.C. - 65 A.D.) whose works contained correct usage and construction, offering the girls profound lessons in the seven virtues. It is reasonable to assume that discussions concerning the principles of morals

Into the seventeenth century it was commonly held that the most suitable occupation for a woman was that of housework. If she would find leisure it was to be occupied in needlepoint or the playing of an instrument. In **The Letter** by Jan Vermeer (1632-1675) the artist emphasizes the play of light on his subjects by showing them through a dark doorway or between curtains—both of which are used here.

would evolve as a natural outgrowth of the girls' readings of both Cicero and Seneca.[20]

Concerning other educational topics, Woodward refers to the first humanist treatise on the education of women written by Leonardo Bruni.[21] Woodward's translation of the treatise reveals that Bruni held that history was a suitable subject for study by girls. Bruni felt that the study of history increased girls' enjoyment of life, by enabling girls to understand the origin and development of their own country. Furthermore, historical studies enabled them to recognize the past achievements of the citizens and rulers, while creating within the girls an appreciation of and for contemporary affairs. Although Bruni approved of history in curriculum development for girls, he considered astronomy, arithmetic and geometry as unfeminine topics and, thereby, rendered them unsuitable and unwholesome for girls and women. In that instance, Bruni emphasized the humanist outlook toward women's education: manners and character were primary; literary erudition was secondary.[22]

To show that the humanists were not in total agreement concerning a curriculum development for Italian Renaissance girls, the viewpoint of Matteo Palmieri (1406-1498)[23] must be considered. In opposition to the Bruni opinion, Palmieri felt that geometry and music trained "the voice and the mind."[24] Vittorino da Feltre, too, was a staunch supporter of the value of music as a suitable subject to be included in a curriculum for girls.

While divergent opinions existed among humanists in regard to the study of music and geometry in girls' educational programs, to the humanist educator, Greek served as the key to the richest treasures of the Renaissance. Thus Greek was studied by girls, while Latin served as the colloquial language, due to the close relationship which existed between the Greek and the Latin during the Renaissance era. Italy's proximity to Greece was an additional factor in the humanist's decision to teach the living language of Italy's neighboring nation. In short, to the Italian Renaissance woman, the study of Greek was what the study of any modern foreign language is to today's woman-student. Since many instances of Greek learning can be found among the achievements of Renaissance women, it is possible to conjecture that their

Vinceno Foppa has given contemporary civilization one of the most tender—and yet dramatic—records of renaissance education: **Reading Cicero**. The young student, deeply engrossed in the writings of the great Latin orator, is oblivious to all surrounding events and noises. Reading Cicero was a classical mainstay of education in the Renaissance—and the mastering of Cicero and other classical authors would nearly assure the scholar a space in royal or ecclesiastical court. By 1500 the study of Plutarch, Quintilian, and Cicero was considered so essential for the well-developed mind that several civic centers were founded as schools in the belief that such education would lead to a more sound morality. The humanist primarily responsible for the ultimate sixteenth century change in attitude towards an eventual universal education was Vergerius (c. 1393), who placed history at the head of all subjects to be studied, followed by moral philosophy and then by eloquence (or, rhetoric). [From the Wallace Collection]

Among the greatest and most articulate champions of education for women was Sir Thomas More (1478-1535; canonized 1935), Lord Chancelor to Henry VIII (1491-1547), King of England. More was the author of numerous works, the best known and loved being *Utopia*. In the above sketch, executed by Hans Holbein (1497-1543), Thomas More is pictured surrounded by his family—all of whom he insisted be educated. The education of his daughters, at first considered scandelous, was quickly accepted by other nobles who put their daughters and sisters in centers of learning, for which More was congratulated by the humanist Erasmus. [Kupferstichkabinett der Oeffentilichen Kanstsammlung Basel Hausaufnahme]

achievements were results obtained from the education of the girls through the instrumentality of the various tutors of that era.

Since the harmonious development of the body and the mind was strongly advocated in the general treatises of the humanist educators, the girls' physical needs also received ample attention. Although girls were spared the inconveniences of war, they were not exempt from the inconveniences that arose from political changes, and even in peaceful periods, necessary journeys were rigorous. Thus discipline in the form of physical stamina was needed. To meet that need, girls had ample outdoor exercises, while the cultivation of the classical dances was also a part of their educational program. To combine physical fitness with academic learning, tutors of the Renaissance era were known to have taken their pupils on horse-back to a sun-filled meadow to hold class sessions.

The moral and religious training of the Renaissance girls was not neglected either. Most humanist educators—by precept as well as by example—promoted religious practice among their pupils. Students and tutors, in a body, attended church regularly and formed habits of piety and virtue by daily attendance at Mass, by frequentation of the sacraments and by sermons and prayers which were recited together. Consequently, a well-rounded education was achieved.[25]

NOTES

[1] Mozans, *op. cit.*, p. 58.

[2] Durant, *loc. cit.*. Cf. L.B. Alberti, *The Family in Renaissance Florence*, trans. and intro. by Renee N. Watkins (Columbia, S.C.: University of South Carolina Press, 1969), pp. 208-217.

[3] Jacob Burckhardt, *Die Kultur der Renaissance in Italien* (Zweiter Band; Leipzig: Alfred Kröner Verlag, 1919), pp. 87-88 states: "Vor allem ist die Bildung des Weibes in den höchsten Ständen wesentlich dieselbe wie beim Manne. Es erregt den Italienern der Renaissance nicht geringste Gedenten, den literarischen und selbst den philogischen Unterricht auf Töchter und Sönne gleichmässig werfen zu lassen."

[4] Prior to the Renaissance it was customary for girls to be wed as young as eight or ten years of age; see Rene La Clavière de Maulde,

The Women of the Renaissance (New York: G.P. Putnam's Sons, 1901), pp. 94-98. Renaissance girls were wed at a somewhat older age: marriage at thirteen or fourteen years was commonplace.

[5]Mozans, *op. cit.*, p. 62.

[6]de Maulde, *op. cit.*, pp. 96-106.

[7]*Ibid.*, p. 264.

[8]Ludovico Dolce, *Della Institutione delle Donne* (Venice, 1547), is a description and analysis on the education of women, as well as a blue-print for the increased intellectualization and purification of women according to set standards.

[9]See below, chap. 3.

[10]de Maulde, *op. cit.*, p. 104.

[11]William Woodward, *Vittorino de Feltre and Other Humanist Educators* (2d ed.; New York: Columbia University Teachers College Press, 1963). Woodward translated four short Latin treatises which had been published between 1400 and 1460 which defined the humanist idea of education during the Italian Renaissance; the treatises and their authors are: Pier Paolo Vergerio, *De ingenius moribus et liberalibus adolescentiae studiis*; Leonardo Bruni, *De Studiis et literis*; Aeneas Sylvius (Pope Pius II), *De liberorum educatione*; and, Battista Guarino, *De ordine docendi et studenti.*

[12]Renaissance man focused his attention on human interests and aspirations. Humanism was the most characteristic intellectual movement of the Renaissance. The humanists emphasized the value of education because they felt that learning led to virtue; the more learned a person was, the more virtuous he was. Since life during the Renaissance was no longer viewed in a rigid, formal manner, education had a wider-ranged out-look than merely concentrating on the ecclesiastical and theological aspects of learning. For that reason Italian humanism leaned toward encouraging individual expression and individual personal development rather than authority. To gain as much satisfaction from life and to be a well-rounded person (*l'uomo universale*) was the Renaissance ideal for which to strive. To achieve that end, humanist educators had a tendency to return to the liberal type education portrayed by such ancients as Aristotle (c. 384-322 B.C.), Plato (c. 427-347 B.C.), Cicero (106-43 B.C.), among others. It is well to note that such men as Leonardo Bruni (1369-1444), Battista Guarino (1434-1513), Guarino da Verona (1374-1460), Vittorino da Feltre (1378-1446), and Juan Luis Vives (1492-1540) basically agreed upon the concept of a liberal education: encompassing encyclopedic facets of reality. Another significant point is that the first humanists were Italian. It is reasonable to

assume then that this factor had a bearing on why Italian women advanced in the educational field more rapidly than did their European counterparts.

There are excellent references for further study on Renaissance humanism, including Georg Voigt, *Die Wiederbelung des Classichen Alterthums, oder das erste Jahrhundert des Humanismus* (2 vols., 2d ed. Berlin: n.p., 1859); William J. Bouwsma, *The Interpretation of Renaissance Humanism* (New York: Macmillan, 1959); Paul Oskar Kristeller, *Renaissance Thought* (2 vols.; New York: Harper Torchbooks, 1965); Wallace K, Ferguson, *The Renaissance in Historical Thought* (Boston: Houghton-Mifflin, 1948). For detailed contemporary arguments, see Erasmus of Rotterdam, *Colloquies*, trans. by N. Bailey (London, 1900), vol. II, pp. 114-119. The German involvement is discussed by J. M. Fletcher, "Wealth and Poverty in the Medieval German Universities," in *Europe in the Late Middle Ages*, ed. by J. R. Hale [et al.], (Evanston, Ill.: Northwestern University Press, 1965), pp. 411-36.

[13] See chap. 1, note 11, above.

[14] *Ibid.*, note 12.

[15] Woodward, *op. cit.*, p. 247.

[16] *Ibid.*, p. 248.

[17] Vittorino da Feltre is discussed in chap. 3, sec. 1, below.

[18] Woodward, *op. cit.*, p. 182.

[19] *Ibid.*, note 2. Cp. Erasmus of Rotterdam, *Christiani matrimoni institutio*: who argues for toil to be moderated with learning: "The distaff is not the only weapon against idleness...it would be better if they taught them to study..." *loc. cit.*.

[20] It is interesting to note, however, that the curriculum development for the subject was different for the girls than for the boys. For the boys, Latin was taught primarily as a medium of thought expression and interpretation. The boys were given selections that prepared them for the practical aspects of life. Since humanist educators sought to establish a framework and the tools by which youth could discover, define, and enlarge upon the meaning, direction and value of their lives, boys read the ancient books. That was because the classics offered the best possible guidance for the youths. For instance, from their readings of Vegetius (4th century A.D.), and Caesar (100-44 B.C.) boys learned the art of warfare; from Virgil (70-19 B.C.) they mastered the techniques of agriculture, while they gained in statesmanship while reading Aristotle's *Politics*. Two excellent primary sources concerning the education of boys are Desiderius Erasmus of Rotterdam's, *The Education of a Christian Prince*, trans. by Lester K. Born (New York: Columbia

University Press, 1936), pp. 139-257; and, Baldessar Castiglione, *The Book of the Courtier*, trans. by Leonard Eckstein Opdycke (New York: Horace Liveright, 1929).

[21] Leonardo Bruni (1369-1444), *De studiis et literis* (Paris, 1642) in Woodward, *op. cit.*, pp. 248-249. In some instances Woodward paraphrased, rather than translated; see the "Biographical Note" by Eugene R. Rice, Jr., p. xvii in the foreword. For Bruni's attitude towards knowledge and education, see his *Rerum suo Tempore Gestarum Commentarius*, in *Muratori Rerum Italicarum Scriptores* XIX, p. 920, where he confessed: "Naturally I burn with love for learning and studied logic and rhetoric," detailing his own career.

[22] Woodward, *ibid.*.

[23] For additional infromation on Palmieri's educational views, see Edward Moore, *Dante and His Early Biographers* (London, 1890), pp. 115-118; cf. John Addington Symonds, *op. cit.*, vol. II, p. 548; and, Lauro Martines, *The Social World of the Florentine Humanists: 1390-1460* (London: Routledge and Kegan Paul, 1963), pp. 138-142, 191-198.

[24] Thomas Frederick Crane, *Italian Social Customs of the Sixteenth Century and Their Influence on the Literature of Europe* (New Haven, Conn.: Yale University Press, 1920), p. 372, quoting from *Della Vita Civile*, the modern reprint of which is *Della vita civile tratto di Mateo Palmieri cittadino Fiorentino* (Milan: Bettoni, 1830). Cp. Agrippa, *De nobilitate et praecellentia foeminei sexus declamatio, loc. cit.* The impact of education was not lost on northern Europe, either: see Johann C. Fusslin, ed., *Beiträge zur Erläuterung der Kirchen Reformations* (Zurich, 1753), vol. 5, p. 213.

[25] It is worth noting that women who were educated under a humanist outlook, tended to embrace the life of the cloister; Albert Hyma, *The Christian Renaissance* (New York: Appleton-Century-Crofts, 1924) addresses this frequently overlooked facet, which is followed up by Roland H. Bainton, *Women of the Reformation in Germany and Italy* (Boston: Beacon Press, 1974), pp. 165-168.

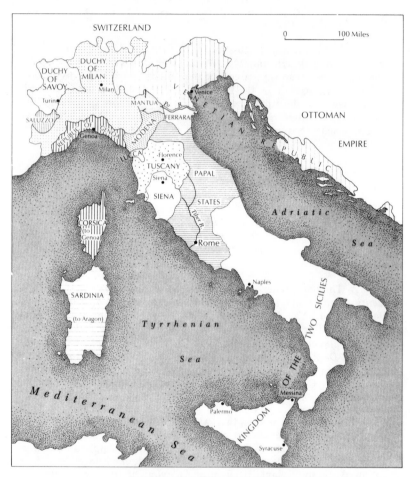

Italy at the Time of Lorenzo de'Medici

CHAPTER THREE

Vittorino and Vives:
The Views and Philosophies of Two Renaissance Humanists

I. The Master of *La Casa Giocasa*

> *...Not everyone is called to be a lawyer, a physician, a philosopher, to live in the public eye, nor has everyone outstanding gifts of natural capacity but all of us are created for the life of social duty, all are responsible for the personal influence which goes forth from us.*
>
> —Vittorino da Feltre

Vittorino da Feltre was "the most remarkable teacher of his day"[1] and he strongly favored the value of a liberal arts education[2] for Renaissance girls and women.[3] Vittorino set up a school at the respected court of the Duke of Mantua, Giovanni Francesco Gonzaga (1466-1519). The school which was called *La casa Giocasa* ("the House of Joy") became known as:[4]

> . . . the first great school of the Renaissance—a school whose spirit, curriculum and method justify us in regarding it as a landmark of cultural importance in the history of classical education. It was indeed the typical school of the Renaissance.

Since Vittorino believed that girls should live virtuous Christian lives, he espoused that girls should be brought up with "all the aids of religion and good example."[5] That Vittorino served as a good example for his students is not disputed: to help the girls establish a firm foundation in Christian attitude and Christian habits, they learned the Psalms and Gospels in their class room and accompanied Vittorino to daily Mass. Following that, they recited the Office of Our Lady together. His reputation as an educator with whom parents could entrust their daughters and sons with utmost confidence, testified to his goodness amid the freedom of sexual promiscuity that was a part of the era.[6] His love for his students was looked upon as saintly, and "all the good in the Christian Renaissance seemed natural to him."[7]

Although Vittorino's love for his pupils was strong and he rarely inflicted corporal punishment on them, he did not coddle his pupils. Rather, he subjected them to the rigors of studying in unheated classrooms during the extreme winters at Mantua. He shared, as did other educators of the era, an aversion to artifical heat. Moreover, regardless of weather conditions, Vittorino advocated regular exercise as the basis for good health which he felt was tantamount to the proper functioning of one's mental processes. Toward that end, two hours of the girls' daily eight hour regimen consisted of mandatory outdoor exercise in which they rode horses and played games that required running, leaping, fencing, and catching balls. In addition to physical exercises Vittorino emphasized the importance of stately bearing and mannerly decorum to his girls since he aimed to "secure the harmonious development of mind, body, and character."[8]

One of Vittorino's techniques for developing and elevating the mind was to surround his pupils with the outstanding art works of the age since "a certain brightness of surroundings conduced [sic] to sound intellectual work."[9] In contrast to the beauty of art works, Vittorino had the Mantuan classroom stripped of its lavish furniture and drapes, thus creating an air of austerity. To increase his students' appreciation of art, Vittorino devoted much of the daily study period to art lessons.

Since Vittorino felt that aesthetics were important to the girls' complete development, he placed heavy emphasis on the role of music in his educational scheme. For that reason, music was an integral part of the mealtime atmosphere at the Mantuan school. Vittorino did, however, alert his pupils to the dangers of listening to what he termed "trivial and worthless"[10] music, lest they take on such qualities themselves. To guard against that occurrence, Vittorino encouraged his students to unite in singing what he considered to be "wholesome" music.[11]

Although Vittorino taught a limited number of girl

students in his school,[12] it appears that he generally followed the same curriculum in their instruction as Bruni had projected in his tract *De studiis et literis.*[13] Since there were no printed books in Vittorino's school he, of necessity, taught by lecture.

Vittorino had won acclaim as a Latinist and was proficient in Greek in conversation and writing.[14] Thus his girl students were educated in both classical languages. In teaching the languages, Vittorino read aloud the classical authors, interjecting brief biographical sketches to whet the students' interest. As he continued reading, he explained not only the language, but also the subject matter, enabling the students to better understand the topic.

It was not unusual for Vittorino's pupils of eleven or twelve years of age to read aloud their own original essays which were written in Latin or Greek. In their reading, they were expected to discuss the meaning of their composition and they expected their pronounciation to be corrected by their master. Since Vittorino placed emphasis on the rote and regurgitation method of learning, girls undoubtedly underwent frequent word-drill sessions, although there is no such reference in existing material. Still, it is known that daily use of Latin enabled students to master the grammar aspects of the language and even students of average intelligence made rapid progress in Latin, as well as in Greek.[15]

Since the individual practice in correct diction and literary composition was an important facet of Vittorino's educational program, he dictated vocabulary words for his students to memorize. Then, to help them master the techniques of the form and the structure of the words, the girls recited, explained, and translated simple passages from the works of classical poets: Ovid (43 B.C. - 18 A.D.), Horace, Virgil, and Lucan. Likewise, Vittorino employed the same methodological approach in presenting the study of history.[16] To Vittorino, history centered around the story of ancient Greece and ancient Rome. To accomplish a significant understanding of events of the past, Vittorino's pupils read the narratives of Cicero, Plutarch, Caesar, and Livy (59 B.C. - 17 A.D.). Since the teachings of specific economic, political, and cultural aspects were not available at that time, Vittorino did not attempt to teach a critical

Maria Portinari. A unique study of Renaissance woman executed by the master artist Hans Memling (1430?-1495) details not only the growing interest in the earthly existence of humankind as demonstrated by the careful attention to her jeweled collar, ring upon her left hand, and the luxury of her rich but durable black broadcloth dress. The portrait also portrays the carry-over of mediaeval psychology as noted in the melancholy sadness (suggestive of the pessimism of northern religious piety) in her sharply intelligent face. Maria Portinari was the wife of Tommaso Portinari, a Florentine citizen who earned a fortune as the representative of the Medici banking interests in Burges, Flanders, who promenaded his earned wealth in his wife's jewelry. (The Metropolitan Museum of Art. Bequest of Benjamin Altman, 1913).

The education of women in the European Renaissance is seen dramatically in **The Money Changer and His Wife** by Quentin Massys (fl. 1514). This portrait is one measure of the West's changing attitudes towards both the growing respectability of such previously "outcast" professions as moneylending, and women's involvement in the world of business. Massys' realistic, richly detailed Flemish style shows that women not only participated in the world of commerce on par with men, but also that women were increasingly literate: as demonstrated by the book laid before the money changer's wife, the books on the shelf behind the couple, and the scale used to determine weight of coin. The artist signs his masterpiece with his own image captured in the small round mirror at the fore.

study of history. Rather, the girls studied biographical treatments of great men of the past. In doing so, Vittorino placed stress on the impct of the individual upon history. Thus, "the study of history then, as a humanist school-master understood it, was the contemplation of noble deeds told by a master of words."[17]

In some respects, Vittorino was an innovative teacher, as he used alphabet letters fashioned from ivory to teach his students to read. Since he regarded arithmetic as "training in accuracy and businesslike form,"[18] he made the subject more interesting by using colored beads to teach the girls how to add sums. In another attempt to pique the students' interest, mathematical games were played. Vittorino's method of guarding against his students becoming fatigued was also relatively innovative—he alternated two hours of study with two hours of exercise, with a meal period serving as a break between morning and afternoon classroom routine.

The later hours in the Mantuan school day were devoted to individual instruction for Vittorino's pupils. During this specific time period, Vittorino gave special attention to his gifted students. By adjusting some of his teaching methods, he enabled his superior students to be challenged to their full potential. In his free evening hours, Vittorino unselfishly devoted time to his students needing tutorial assistance.

Unselfishness appears to be but one facet of the character of this famous educator whom historians generally agree was also gentle, deeply religious, charitable, and devoid of personal ambition and envy. He was fully involved in devoting himself to his students. Above all, he was a modest man who "left no writings behind him, giving it as his opinion that the ancients had already written enough."

II. The Spaniard in the English Court

...Learning is the truest food of the mind. Hence, it is not proper for the body to be nourished and the mind to be kept hungry; for from the latter springs all that is pleasurable or delightful, secure, or long-lasting. In studies, one branch gives birth to another, and each renews itself; nor do they ever leave us, or ever make us weary.

—Juan Luis Vives

Juan Luis Vives is considered to be one of the foremost progressive educators of the Renaissance and symbolic of the humanist cause. He stressed the importance of education and the perfecting of the individual's learning, wisdom, and ethics. Vives felt that learning was pure and worthwhile only if it led to virtue. According to Vives, by using one's intelligence to weigh the nature and value of each experience, one determines the course to follow (virtue) and the course to avoid (evil).[20]

Vives also believed that learning was formed by means of intelligence, memory, and study, while intelligence develops and becomes finely honed by practice. Similarly, Vives felt that memory improves by exercising it, while idleness leads to the decay of memory. To guard against such decadence, Vives advocated that students perform two functions prior to retiring each night: first, in solitude, recall to memory each thing that has been heard, seen, read, or accomplished that day; second, when desiring to commit to memory a specific passage or lesson, read the specific word(s) several times immediately prior to retiring. Upon arising in the morning, recall the word(s) to memory.[21]

To emphasize the fact that memory wants and needs work to do, Vives urged his students to put their memories to test on a daily basis. Vives explained that memory has matters committed to its care. The matter is then guarded by the memory and it is nourished by a continual refreshment of the stored matter. Eventually the memory, on demand, will relinquish custody of the deposited matter for the individual's use.[22]

In regard to concentration, Vives encouraged students not to let their minds wander when reading or listening lest they lose time and labor. Moreover, he urged students to cast aside any considerations that would distract their minds from their own studies. Should the student's mind veer from her reading, "call it back again. . . with a little word."[23]

In conjuction with memorizing and concentrating, Vives advised all students to carry a notebook at all times. By doing so, the student was able to record daily the meaningful things which she had heard or read. Vives cautioned, however, not to accumulate words for the sake of having a lengthy vocabulary, but to understand the meaning of each

Queen Mary I (1516-1558)

Mary Tudor, the daughter of Henry VIII and
Catherine of Aragon, before she became Queen of
England (1553-1558) spent her time in literary
pursuits since she was, for most of her life,
required to spend it in seclusion away from the
court. During this period of time she mastered
several languages (including French, Greek, and
Latin), completed a translation of the New Testament, and romanced the idea of being in love with
her cousin Phillip of Spain (Phillip II) who she
would later marry as Queen. Although personally
popular, and especially loved since she was the
daughter of Catherine, she alienated her most
powerful subjects by marrying Phillip and bringing
England back into the Roman Catholic fold.

word. Not only did the notebook serve to enhance a student's vocabulary, it also enabled the girl to perfect her writing style, which in turn, served as an aid to eloquent speech. The notebook, in effect, became the student's personal grammar textbook containing not only meaningful words and concepts, but also systematically arranged examples of accepted usage.[24]

Vives had further views on the education of girls which he expressed in *De Institutione Feminae Christianae* (1523), which placed heavy stress on obedience.[25] The reason for that emphasis was Vives' feelings that women's place was in the home; thus, she should excel in such virtues as obedience, piety, and modesty.

In Vives' compendium on women's education, he remarked that girls should be taught by women, although women educators were the exception rather than the rule during the Renaissance era.[26] Vives also recommended that contrary to the customs of the period, girls should be taught in their native tongue, rather than in Latin. Inasmuch as Vives' philosophy for educating girls revolved around the "training for domestic life, in which the mother should be distinguished by the deepest culture of piety and all the intellectual education conducive to religious development,"[27] he encouraged religious training by recommending that girls recite their prayers in the vernacular.

To show the emphasis which was placed on the education of Renaissance girls, consider these facts: in 1523, Vives wrote, in addition to his *De Instructione Feminae Christianae*, a short study plan for Mary Tudor (1516-1588);[28] and in 1524 wrote *Satellitium* or *Symbola*,[29] to be used also in the education of the young Princess Mary Tudor. Thus in the space of one year, Vives had written three books on the education of Renaissance women. In contrast, throughout the Middle Ages, only seven books which dealt with women's education had been published in England. Of that total, two of the works were written in Latin.

Vives study plan for Mary Tudor was his philosophic proto-type for girls' education. The outline was an in-depth prospectus and syllabus of authors which Vives had synthesized and used in teaching grammar, penmanship, pronunciation, memorization, vocabulary, and Latin conversa-

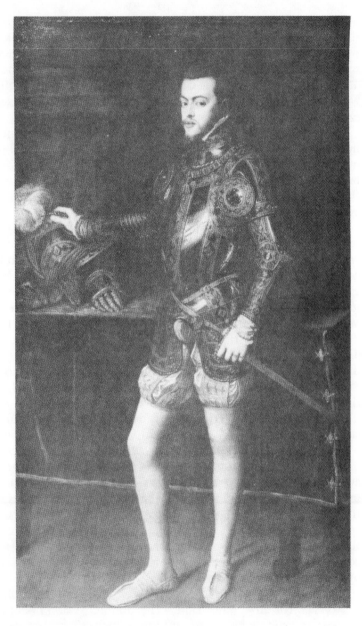

Philip II, by Titian. Painted when Philip was 24, this picture was sent to Mary Tudor, Queen of England, so that she would recognize her future husband. (Courtesy *Museo del Prado,* Madrid)

tion. Included in Vives' study plan were concepts of such classical and contemporary writers as Plutarch (46-120 A.D.), Cato the Elder (234-149 B.C.), Seneca (c. 3 B.C. - 65 A.D.), Erasmus (1466-1536), and Melancthon (1497-1560). Vives selected those authors not only for their works, but for the fact that each had lived in a moral manner. Thus, they became examples of virtue for young Princess Mary.

The instructions which accompanied the study guide for the then seven year old Mary Tudor, exemplified Vives' attitude of combining learning with ethics. He warned that Mary should not be taught improper or disgraceful matters. Moreover, Vives recommended that this young princess be taught in the company of three or four carefully selected peers, rather than being taught alone. Vives admonished—gently—however, that Mary Tudor be among fellow-students who are "most piously and liberally educated, from whom she will not hear or learn anything to injure her morals; for conduct aught to be the first care."[30]

In Vives' *Satellitium*, the 239 maxims or mottoes it contained for Mary Tudor, were to serve "as a body-guard for the child's mind."[31]   It was Vives' opinion that if the young princess heeded the advice contained within the *Satellitium*, the 239 guards (maxims/mottoes) would protect her. He cautioned Mary, however, never to get farther than one finger's breadth from the advice contained in the book. In that remark, Vives again evinced the stress that he placed on obedience in young girls.

The fact that Mary Tudor was educated in a wide-range of subjects was not unusual for girls of wealthy families. In fact, Vives advocated a rigorous "regimen of work with a course of cold water and a vegetable diet"[32] to deter girls from becoming vain and thinking of marriage at an early age.   However, Vives did advocate that to prepare young girls for marriage that the practical arts of "plain cooking, of domestic economy or the common medicines"[33] be part of every girl's education. His general educational goal for girls "was the development through letters and moral teaching of the high-principled lady, wife, and mother who would become the intelligent companion and mistress of the household."[34]

NOTES

[1]Crane, *op. cit.*, p. 164. Cf. Burkhardt, *op. cit.*, p. 127, and Symonds, *op. cit.*, pp. 209-216. Maud F. Jerrold, *Italy in the Renaissance* (London: Meuthen, 1927), p. 71, states that Vittorino was "one of the most remarkable schoolmasters the world has seen." For details on Vittorino's prowess as an educator, see *ibid.*, pp. 71-83.

[2]The liberal arts curriculum consisted of the *trivium* (grammar, rhetoric, and dialectic), and the *quadrivium* (arithmetic, geometry, astronomy, and music).

[3]Frank Pierrepont Graves, *A History of Education During the Middle Ages and the Transition to Modern Times* (New York: Macmillan, 1910), pp. 126-127.

[4]John E. Wise, *The History of Education* (New York: Sheed and Ward, 1964), p. 156.

[5]*Ibid.*, Additional details on the Christian character of Vittorino are in Jerrold, *op. cit.*, pp. 75-76, 81.

[6]Symonds, *op. cit.*, p. 211.

[7]Wise, *loc. cit.*. Graves, *loc. cit.*, states that Vittorino taught a variety of subjects, although he taught them with "a different relative importance and a new interpretation as to content" carrying through his special Christian humanism in the process.

[8]Woodward, *op. cit.*, p. 36. Vittorino's concern for the "harmonious development of the mind, body and character" was not unique; it was the goal of each humanistic educator. Cf. Symonds, *op. cit.*, pp. 212-213 for an additional description of students' outdoor exercise periods. An interesting sidenote concerning the students' outdoor activities is found in Jerrold, *op. cit.*, p. 75, who comments "Vittorino, wiry, active, and indefatigable, took part in everything."

[9]Woodward, *op. cit.*, p. 32.

[10]William Woodward, *Studies in Education During the Age of the Renaissance: 1400-1600* (New York: Russell and Russell, 1965), p. 20.

[11]*Ibid.*.

[12]Jerrold, *op. cit.*, p. 73; Woodward, *loc. cit.*; Wise, *loc. cit.*.

[13]See above, chap. 3.

[14]In 1396, Vittorino studied Latin at Padua under Giovanni da Ravenna (fl. 1350-1400), the protege of Petrarch. Vittorino learned Greek from his friend, the famed educator, Guarino da Verona, and in turn Vittorino shared his Latin expertise with Guarino. Cf. Symonds, *The Revival of Learning*, pp. 209-210. Jerrold, *Italy in the Renaissance*, p. 71, states that Vittorino "was the finest Latin scholar of the time." Cf. Graves, *op. cit.*, p. 123 for a discussion of Vittorino's training in the home of Gasparino da Barzizza (1370-1431), called "the greatest of living Latinists."

[15]Symonds, *op. cit.*, p. 214, discusses Vittorino's dependence upon his students "learning by heart and repetition, as the surest means of forming a good style." Woodward, *op. cit.*, p. 45.

[16]*Ibid.*, note 1 states "This information is derived from Sassuola da Prato (fl. 1450) a very good authority on points of this kind. He was pupil [sic] at Mantua between 1437 and 1443; and for some time was assistant to Vittorino." Woodward further remarks, in note 2, that in regard to the simple passage of historical narrative Vittorino taught his students: "Sassuola compiled a little book, which contained a selection of such passages in Latin and Greek; it is unfortunate not now to be traced at Mantua, no doubt it represents the method pursued by Vittorino himself." Cf. Jerrold, *op. cit.*, pp. 80-82, for other writings of Vittorino's students which concern Vittorino's methodology.

[17]Woodward, *op. cit.*, p. 17.

[18]*Ibid.*, p. 42; cf. Jerrold, *op. cit.*, pp. 78-79.

[19]*Ibid.*, p. 82. Cf. Woodward, *op. cit.* p. 14; Wise, *loc. cit.*. Cp. Edward J. Power, *Main Currents in History of Education* (New York: McGraw-Hill, 1962), pp. 285-289 for an additional evaluation of Vittorino's contribution to Renaissance education.

[20]Vives' thoughts concerning learning, virtue, and ethics are detailed in Marian Leona Tobriner, ed., *Vives' Introduction to Wisdom: A Renaissance Textbook* (New York: Columbia University Teachers College Press, 1968), pp. 85-110. Vives' contemporaries linked his name with More and Erasmus for having written many treatises illustrating social conceptions of humanists.

[21]*Ibid.*, pp. 103-108, nos. 141-143, 185, 188.

[22]*Ibid.*, p. 107, nos. 183, 184.

[23]*Ibid.*, p. 103, no. 145.

[24]*Ibid.*, p. 106, nos. 172, 173.

[25]This famous treatise was dedicated by Vives to Catherine of Aragon (1485-1536), and was translated from Latin into English in 1529 by Richard Hyrde, tutor to the household of Thomas More. The work became the accepted theoretical manual on women's education in the sixteenth century, and won for Vives the prestigious title of being called a "second Quintillian."

[26]Authorities disagree about Vives' preference for women educators to teach girls. Juan Luis Vives, *Vives: "On Education": A Translation of the* De Tradendis Disciplinis *of Juan Luis Vives*, trans. by Foster Watson, foreword by Francesco Cordasco (Newark, N.J.: Rowman and Littlefield, 1971), foreword, iii; and, Wise, *op. cit.*, p. 182, agrees that Vives advocated women teachers for girls. Woodward, *op. cit.*, p. 208, qualifies his opinion by stating that Vives preferred "if such may be found, a woman teacher." De Maulde, *op. cit.*, p. 98, flatly states that Vives "insisted upon instruction by men."

[27]Vives, *op. cit.*, pp. xiv-xv; cf. Eugene F. Rice, Jr., *The Renaissance Idea of Wisdom* (Cambridge, Mass.: Harvard University Press, 1958), pp. 160-162.

[28]Juan Luis Vives, *De Ratione Studii Puerlis*; cf. Vives, *Vives and the Renaissance Education of Women*, ed. Foster Watson (New York: Longmans, Green, & Co., 1912), pp. 48-55.

[29]*Satellitium* or *Symbola* is also known as *Satellitium Animi*.

[30]Vives, *op. cit.*, foreword, iii.

[31]*Ibid.*.

[32]De Maulde, *op. cit.*, p. 93.

[33]*Ibid.*

[34]R. Freeman Butts, *A Cultural History of Education* (New York: McGraw-Hill, 1947), p 228; cf. Willystine Goodsell, *A History of the Family As A Social and Educational Institution* (New York: Macmillan, 1930), p. 289. Cp. Power, *op. cit.*, pp. 300-302, for a further account of Vives impact on education. With the coming of the Reformation much of this, unfortunately, was done away with and the advances of the Renaissance shelved for centuries.

CHAPTER FOUR

The Erudite Lady of Mantua and the Diplomat of Milan

The birth of Isabella d'Este (1474-1539) caused no overt excitement; the birth of her younger sister, Beatrice d'Este (1475-1497), aroused even less enthusiasm. They were not the hoped for heirs of Ercole I (1431-1505), undisputed ruler of the Ferrara court: "The advent of a girl was little welcomed, and the rejoicings for the birth of a female princess were usually of a feeble character..."[1]

Despite the disadvantages of being females, the d'Este girls were born at a time when it was realized that education was of prime importance to both males and females. The fact that they were born into a noble family, plus the availability to them of an education equal to that of boys of upper-strata families, enabled the d'Este sisters to reach significant heights of erudition during their lifetime.

From the time that her two daughters were small girls, Duchess Leonora of Ferrara (1457?-1493) knew that one day both Isabella and Beatrice would preside over courts of their own. This foregone conclusion was a result of Isabella, at age six, being promised in marriage to Francesco Gonzaga (1466-1519), son of the Marquis of Mantua Frederico I (1441-1484). Similarly at the age of five, Beatrice was betrothed to Lodovico Sforza (1451-1508),[2] then the Duke of Bari, later the Duke of Milan. Since Renaissance women of the upper social strata were expected to rule the domain in the absence of their husbands, as well as to form decisions of a political nature, it is understandable that the Duchess Leonora sought exceptionally fine educations for both of her two daughters.

Leonora had no problem in acquiring the services of learned scholars to tutor her young daughters. The cultivation of art, science, and learning had led the University of Ferrara to become the most distinguished institute of learning in Renaissance Italy. Hence, around 1485, the formal education of Isabella and Beatrice d'Este began with Battista Gaurino (1434-1513)[3] being selected to provide a classical foundation for their studies. Under his tutelage and guidance, the girls read Virgil and Cicero, studied the history of Rome and Greece, and the grammar of Manuel Chrysolaras (c. 1355-1415).

Languages figured prominently in the education of the d'Este sisters. Latin and French were studied, with Isabella excelling in Latin,[4] but with neither girl achieving fluency in French. Since mastering Italian poetry and literature came easily to the girls, their tutor then exposed them to the recitations of leading Renaissance poets. While they were listening to the poets' writings the girls were also busily engaged in needlework, at which they became adept.

It is reasonable to conjecture that while the girls' hands were occupied with their needlecraft, their eyes were absorbing the beauties which surrounded them.[5] Similarly, it is conceivable that their ears frequently were attuned to the various topics that were being discussed by their father and the learned scholars and advisors who frequented the Ferrara court. Since they were being raised in an atmosphere of art and learning, it is natural to assume that the d'Este sisters found inspiration at Ferrara, while also developing the ability to interpret thoughts and feelings in the forms of beauty which shaped their environments. It is fair also to presume that such an aesthetic education led Isabella to become the acute critic and life-long patron of the arts that she was. Likewise, it is probable that listening to the recitations of poets in her childhood study periods influenced Beatrice to present similar recitations as a form of entertainment in the Milan court. Perhaps that same influence led her to acquire youthful foreign poets as proteges of her court.

In conjuction with their academic studies, the d'Este sisters were studying music, dancing, and learning the social graces. Isabella was but a toddler when her dancing lessons began, with her singing lessons commencing shortly thereafter. When she was a young matron, Isabella was quick to charm guests of the Mantuan Court with the beauty of her voice and her musical talents. In fact, both girls became excellent dancers and distinguished musicians whose talents on the claricord (or clavicord), viol, and the lute brought them acclaim.[6]

Horsemanship and outdoor sports formed another aspect of the education of the young d'Este sisters. These activities were especially appealing to Beatrice, leading her to become an accomplished equestrienne and huntswoman. After her marriage, Beatrice gained renown for fearlessly hunting wild boar and indulging in falconry and hawking. The following portion of a letter written to Isabella by Beatrice is indicative of her zeal for hunting:[7]

> We are enjoying warm and splendid weather, and every day we go riding with the dogs and falcons and my husband and I never come home without having enjoyed ourselves exceedingly in hunting herons and other waterfowl. .... Game is so plentiful here that hares are to be seen jumping out at every corner. Indeed, the eye cannot take in all that one desires to see, and it is scarcely possible to count up the number of animals which are to be seen in this neighbourhood. ....

Although Beatrice had time for such pleasures as the hunt, performing important duties was another facet of her life as the Duchess of Bari. In 1493, Beatrice began undertaking a leading role in political affairs by serving as Lodovico's ambassador and spokeswoman before the Doge and Signoria of Venice. In speaking before the Signory in the Doge's Sala del Collegio, Beatrice presented Lodovico's pending plan to unite with the King of France, Charles VIII (1470-1498), to invade the city-states of the northern republics.[8] It was Lodovico's hope that the Venetian Republic would join the alliance, and to that end, the diplomatic and charming Beatrice was sent to address the councillors. Although the value and quality of Beatrice's education were obvious to her listeners,the Signory, who admired her rare courage, eloquence, and the erudition of the eighteen year old duchess, declined to commit themselves to Lodovico's plan.[9]

In May, 1495, Lodovico, considered to be courageous and held in high esteem by his peers and subjects, was crowned Duke of Milan. Within one week of his coronation,

60

Allegory of Good Government, by Lorenzetti, Siena.

it was to be Beatrice's astuteness and intelligence that saved the Duke from disgrace. When news of an impending attack on Milan by Louis, duc d'Orleans (1462-1515), reached Lodovico, he reacted in an unusual manner: he lost his nerve, fled the city, and was incapable of coping with the situation. Beatrice's actions were the antithesis demonstrated by her husband. Showing courage and resolve, Beatrice sent for the nobles and arranged for the defense of the capital city.

Although the Duke of Milan soon recovered his aplomb, from that day forward, Beatrice began accompanying her husband to political meetings. One such meeting was the peace-seeking conference with the French, whose king, Charles VIII, had conquered Naples.[10] At that conference in Vercelli, near Novaro, the French commissioners were astounded by the young woman's intelligence and under-standing of the matter at hand. Unfortunately, at twenty-two years of age, Beatrice died in childbirth while being de-livered of a still-born son. Thus, the full potential of the young duchess never fully developed.

Although Beatrice's death was premature, Isabella enjoyed a long, productive lifespan, during which she con-tinually sought to acquire learning. Following her marriage on 11 February 1490, it was Isabella's intention to further her education. However, she soon learned that affairs of the Mantuan Court consumed much of her time. It was at the urging of Battista Guarino that the young Duchess sent for a tutor[11] after Battista declared the continuance of her educa-tion would bring Isabella fame "since a truly educated woman is as rare as a phoenix."[12] That Isabella was a "truly educated woman" is revealed in the innumerable letters that she wrote concerning such a wide range of subjects: affairs of state, discoveries in the New World, *objets d'art* critiques, and commentaries on the fashions of the day. Isabella's read-ing matter further reflected upon her education. Her library included the works of Livy, Homer, Virgil, Pliny, fifteenth century Italian translations of Greek and Hebrew literature, even religious works of all eras. It is interesting to note that the d'Este sisters, like other girls of the period enjoyed the bawdy romances of Boccaccio.

Isabella remained a voracious reader even though she was involved in presiding over the Mantuan Court in her husband's absence. The following letter to Zorzo Brognolo is but one of the many letters written by Isabella[13] which reveals her deep interest in reading:[14]

> ...We wish to ask all the booksellers in Venice for a list of all the Italian books in prose or verse containing battle stories and fables of heroes in modern or ancient times, more especially those which relate to the Paladins of France ....

No facet of Isabella's education was neglected in her adult years. In 1491, her love of music led her to master the art of playing the lyre and to resume her singing lessons with Giovanni Martini (fl. 1480). The vocal lessons were augmented by additional coaching for Isabella by Girolamo da Sestola (?1510-?1580), the Ferrarese musician.

The same year, with an almost insatiable appetite for music stirring in her soul, Isabella ordered a silver lute from the famed musician Atalanti Migliorotti (fl. 1490). The lute became Isabella's favorite musical instrument, serving as the instrument on which she accompanied herself, playing and singing with grace and skill.[15]

Although both the d'Este sisters musical talents had a pleasing effect on their listeners, it is the many letters written by Isabella,[16] combined with those of Beatrice that serve as an historical record of the education each received. Their letters contain news of social, political, and cultural events. Many of Isabella's letters give evidence of her motherly instincts and her solid piety—characteristics coveted in Italian Renaissance women. One letter exemplifies both of these traits. With motherly pride she writes of her first-born son, Frederico (1500-1540) as he was playing near-by while she was reciting the Office. The encouragement that she gave two of her daughters, Livia (1497?-1508), and Ippolita (1503-1580) in their religious education and vocation is further testimony that Isabella d'Este raised her children in a pious and loving atmosphere. In other letters, Isabella wrote of attending Masses and participating in pilgrimages as well as visiting churches and convents.

The Marchesa pursued art with a zeal equal to her literary endeavors. Isabella spent over three years (1499-1502) attempting to restore the statue of Virgil to its place of honor

"St. James on the Way to His Execution," a fresco by Andrea Mantegna, is innovative in its perspective and use of classical models. St. James, at the left, is shown blessing a Roman soldier and healing a paralytic. Mantegna's interest in historical detail is obvious in both the classical buildings and the costumes of the soldiers.

in Mantua. Although her efforts proved fruitless, Mantuan officials proposed that Isabella's name appear at the base of the statue.[17]   The Marchesa also spent considerable effort attempting to obtain a torso of an ancient marble statue of Venus, as well as Michaelangelo Buonarroti's

Lady with a Nose-Gay by Andrea del Verrocchio (1435-1488)

"Sleeping Cupid."[18]

In 1492, to further her education in art, as well as to surround herself with aesthetic beauty, Isabella commissioned the services of Andrea Mantegna (1431-1506) who

Part of the Triumphs of Julius Caesar, by Mantegna, Hampton Court.

had been the Gonzaga family painter for three generations. The great Mantegna enhanced the walls of the Mantuan Court's Chapel and Gallery with the likeness of Francesco's Arabian horses, as well as the paintings of hawks and falcons. Montegna became but one of the many talented artists for whom Isabella served as patron and friend throughout her lifetime.

It was also in 1492 that Isabella retained Giovanni Santi (1435-1494) the father of the famed artist Raphael, to paint a series of family portraits to hang in the Mantuan Court.[19]

While Isabella was actively engaged in the pursuit of knowledge, especially in the field of language, music, and art, she was also contributing to the governing of Mantua. In 1494-1495, despite the pressures involved in presiding over the court while Francesco was absent engaging in military skirmishes, Isabella was handling the affairs of Mantua with aplomb. Her wisdom, judiciousness, and intelligence won her

Colleoni, Venice, by Verrocchio. (Courtesy, The Bettmann Archive)

the admiration of the Mantuan advisors to the court.

Again in 1496, the Marquis being involved in military pursuits, Isabella was left to care for the affairs of state.[20] Still she found the time to continue the pursuit of her classical studies, applying herself, in consultation with Ercole Strozzi (1462-1531), the Ferrara artist and humanist, to the mastery of Latin grammar. In addition, Isabella acquired the services of the young musician Angelo Testagrossa for further lessons on the lute.[21]

Isabella's thirst for knowledge did not slacken and in 1504, she broadened her classical studies by again studying grammar. Undoubtedly Isabella's education contributed to her astuteness, sagacity, and wisdom in the many political intrigues involving her husband. Isabella's diplomatic involvement, which covered a lengthy span of years is well summarized by Julia Cartwright:[22]

By her skillful diplomacy this able woman saved a state of Mantua from falling a prey to the ambitious designs of Caesare Borgia, or the vengeance of two powerful French monarchs Louis XII. and Francis I. At the same time she helped her brother, Duke Alphonso of Ferrara, to resist the furious assults of Julius II. and the tortuous policy of Leo X., and to preserve his duchy in the face of the most pro-longed—and determined opposition. . . .

NOTES

[1]William Boulting, *Women in Italy* (New York: Bretano's, 1910), pp. 164-165.

[2]The dark complected Lodovico was also called *Il Moro* because of his resemblance to one of a Moorish background.

[3]Battista Guarino was the son of the famed Guarino de Verona. Battista was succeeded by Japoco Gallino (fl. 1490). The literary coterie that assembled under his direction would carry his ideas on education to most of the courts of Europe, as was most especially the case with Tito Strozzi.

[4]Cartwright, *op. cit.*, vol. I, p. 9, and vol. II, p. 381.

[5]For a description of the paintings, frescoes, and tapestries which adorned the walls of the Ferrara palaces and villas, and descriptions of the silver services, furnishings, and interior decor, see *ibid.*, vol. I, pp. 12-16.

[6]Isabella's first dancing instructor was Ambrogio da Urbino (fl. 1485), and both girls were later taught by dancemaster Lorenzo Lavagnolo (fl. 1485). Cartwright, *A Study of Beatrice d'Este, op. cit.*, p. 37, gives the details. Don Giovanni Martini, the choirmaster of the Ferrara chapel, was the first in a series of music teachers for Isabella, see Cartwright, *Isabella d'Este, op. cit.*, vol. I, pp. 10-11. Cp. Stefano Davari, *Musica in Mantova* (Mantova: Rivista Storica, 1885), p. 61.

[7]Hare, *op. cit.*, p. 119.

[8]Plumb, *op. cit.*, pp. 76-77.

[9]Cotterill, *op. cit.*, pp. 295-297.

[10]*Ibid.*, pp. 297-300 for a discussion of the political relationship between the Duke of Milan and Charles VIII. Cf. Plumb, *op. cit.*, pp. 63-68.

[11]Intially a Mantuan scholar, Sigismondo Golfo (fl. 1490) tutored Isabella but was replaced by Nicco Panizzato (fl. 1490) who was a lecturer at the University of Ferrara. Cf. Cartwright, *op. cit.*, pp. 66-67.

[12]*Ibid.*.

[13]Brognolo (fl. 1490) was the Mantuan envoy to Venice during Francesco Gonzaga's reign. Cf. Cartwright, *ibid.*, vol. II, pp. 20-26.

[14]*Ibid.*, , vol. I, p. 76. An explanation for Isabella's interest in military campaign history can be offered on the basis of her husband's interest: Lodovico carried a copy of Caesar's *Commentaries* on his campaigns.

[15]On Isabella's musical talents, see A. Luzio and R. Renier, *Niccolo da Correggio* (Torino: Gionale Storico della Letteratura Italiana, 1893), p. 243.

[16]Isabella wrote over 2000 letters which are currently contained in the State Archives of Mantua.

[17]The proposed inscription was: *Publius Virgilius Mantuanus, Isabella Marchionessa Mantuae restituit.* Cf. Armand Baschet, *Recherches de Documents d'art et l'Histoire dans les Archives Mantoue* (Paris: Gazette des Beaux Arts, 1866), p. 481.

[18]The statues had been taken from the Montefeltri palace in Urbino by Caesare Borgia (1476-1507) when he and his army captured the palace on 21 June 1502. Isabella wrote a diplomatically phrased letter to her brother, Cardinal Ippolito d'Este (1479-1520), in which she requested that he ask the Borgia for the antiques. Her letter ultimately led to the delivery in Mantua of the coveted statues, which arrived on 22 July 1502. See Cartwright, *op. cit.*, vol. I, pp. 230-234, and vol. II, pp. 1-19, for details concerning various antiques, statues, and medals acquired by Isabella for her famous "Studio of the Grotto". Cp. Hare, *op. cit.*, pp. 161-162.

[19]Mantegna's paintings of the Arabian horses are still visible on the walls; see Anna de Koven, *Women in the Cycles of Culture* (New York: G.P. Putnam's Sons, 1941), pp. 100-101. Mantegna's works which hung in the Chapel were presumed to be "Triptych" which contained the "Adoration," as well as the "Death of the Virgin". Cf. Cartwright, *op. cit.*, vol. I, pp. 89-93 for information on the works of Mantegna and other artists at the Mantuan court.

[20]On Isabella's role in conjunction with Francesco's involvement with Lodovico Sforza, see Louis Pelissier, *Les Armies de Ludovico Sforza* (Paris: Revue Historique, 1891). Cp. Cartwright, *op. cit.*, vol. I, pp. 117-124, and vol. II, pp. 31-49.

[21]Isabella engaged Angelo Testagrossa (fl. 1495) whose vocal talents and skill in playing the lute and clavicord had won him acclaim in Milan.

[22]Cartwright, *ibid.*, vol. I, pp. vii-viii. A continuation of this thought is the forthcoming book by Arthur Frederick Ide, *Woman in the Italian Renaissance.*

The Corporal Works of Mercy, by Della Robbia.

BIBLIOGRAPHY

Primary Sources:

Alberi, E., ed., *Relazioni degli ambasciartori veneti al senato.* 15 vols. (Florence, 1839-1863).

Alberti, L. B. *The Family in Renaissance Florence*, trans. intro. by Renee N. Watkins (Columbia, S.C.: University of South Carolina Press, 1969).

Agrippa. *De nobilitate et praecellentia foeminei sexus declamatio* (Paris, 1713).

Aubigne. *Oeuvres complete*, ed. by E. Reaume and F. de Caussade (Paris, 1873), vol. I.

Bruni, Leonardo. *De studiis et literis.* (Cambridge [Eng.] : University Press, 1905).

de Pisan, Christine. *Cyte of Ladyes*, trans. by B. Anslay (London, 1521), Bk. 1, chap. 11, and Bk. 2.

Dolce, Ludivico. *Della Institutione delle Donne* (Venice, 1547).

Erasmus, Desiderius. *Christiani matrimonii institutio* (Basel, 1526).

Erasmus, Desiderius. *Colloquies*, trans. by N. Bailey. 3 vols. (London, 1900).

Erasmus, Desiderius. *The Education of a Christian Prince*, trans. by Lester K. Born (New York: Columbia University Press, 1936).

da Guarino, Battista. *De ordine docendi et studendi* (Verona, 1459).

Machiavelli, Niccolò. *History of Florence* (New York: The Colonial Press, 1901)

Marsiglio of Padua. "Defensor Paci," in *Marsilius of Padua*, 2 vols., ed by Alan Gewirth (New York: Columbia University Press, 1951, 1956).

Palmieri, Matteo. *Della Vita Civile*. (Florence, 1529).

Sylvanius, Aeneas. *De Liberorum Educatione*, intro. and trans. by Joel Stanislaus Nelson (Washington, D.C.: The Catholic University of America Press, 1940).

Vergerio, Pier Paolo. *De ingenius moribus et Liberalibus adolescentiae studiis* (New York: Columbia University Press, 1964).

Vives, Juan Luis. *De Institutione Feminae Christianae* (London, 1523).

Vives, Juan Luis. *De Ratione Studii Puerlis* (London: Gregg Press reprint, 1964).

Vives, Juan Luis. *Satellitum* (London, 1524).

Vives, Juan Luis. *Vives:* "On Education": *A Translation of the* De Trandenis Disciplinis *of Juan Luis Vives*, trans. by Foster Watson; foreword by Francesco Cordasco (Newark, N.J.: Rowman and Littlefield, 1971).

Vives, Juan Luis. *Vives and the Renaissance Education of Women*, ed. by Foster Watson (New York: Longmans, Green and Co., 1912).

Secondary Works:

Bainton, Roland H. *Christendom* (New York: Harper Torchbooks, 1966) vol. I.

Bainton, Roland H. *Women of the Reformation in Germany*

and Italy. (Boston: Beacon Press, 1974).

Beard, Mary R. *Women as Force in History*. (3rd ed.; New York: Collier Books, 1973).

Boulting, William. *Women in Italy* (New York: Bretano's, 1910).

Bouwsma, William J. *The Interpretation of Renaissance Humanism* (New York: Macmillan, 1959).

Burkhardt, Jacob. *Die Kultur der Renaissance in Italien* (Zweit. Bd.; Leipzig: Alfred Kröner Verlag, 1919); and, its translation cited under the title *The Civilization of the Renaissance in Italy*, trans. by S.C.C. Middlemore (2d ed.; London: The Phaidon Press, 1944).

Capponi, G.A. *Storia della Republica di Firenze* 2 vols. (Florence, 1875).

Cartwright, Julia. *Beatrice d'Este, Duchess of Milan, 1475-1497: A Study of the Renaissance* (London: J. M. Dent, 1912).

Cartwright, Julia. *Isabella d'Este, Marchioness of Mantua, 1474-1539: A Study of the Renaissance* (New York: E.P. Dutton, 1903).

Cotterill, H.B. *Italy from Dante to Tasse: 1300-1600.* (New York: Frederick A. Stokes, 1919).

Crane, Thomas Frederick. *Italian Social Customs of the Sixteenth Century and Their Influence on the Literature of Europe* (New Haven, Conn.: Yale University Press, 1920).

Davari, Stefano. *Musica in Mantova* (Mantova: Rivista Storica, 1885).

Durant, Will. *The Renaissance*; vol. 5 of *The Story of Civilization* (New York: Simon and Schuster, 1953).

Eckstein, Lena. *Women Under Monasticism* (Cambridge [Eng.] : University Press, 1896).

Ferguson, Wallace K. *The Renaissance in Historical Thought* (Boston: Houghton-Mifflin Co., 1948).

Gage, Matilda J. *Women, Church and State* (New York: The Truth Seekers Co., 1893).

Gail, Marzieh. *Life in the Renaissance* (New York: Random House, 1968).

Goodsell, Willystine. *A History of the Family As a Social and Educational Institution* (New York: Macmillan, 1930).

Graves, Frank Pierrepont. *A History of Education During the Middle Ages and the Transition to Modern Times* (New York: Macmillan, 1910).

Hare, Christopher [Mrs. Marian Andrews]. *The Most Illustrious Ladies of the Renaissance* (London: Harper & Bros., 1911).

Harsburgh, E.L.S. *Lorenzo the Magnificent and Florence in Her Golden Age* (London, 1909).

Hyma, Albert. *The Christian Renaissance* (New York: Appleton-Century-Crofts, 1924).

Ide, Arthur Frederick. *Woman in the Italian Renaissance* [ms. (in press)].

Jerrold, Maud F. *Italy in the Renaissance* (London: Menthuen, 1927).

Jerrold, Maud F. *Vittoria Colonna: With Some Account of Her Friends and Her Times* (New York: Books for Libraries Press, 1969).

de Koven, Anna. *Women in Cycles of Culture* (New York: G.P. Putnam's Sons, 1941).

Kristeller, Paul Oskar. *Renaissance Thought: The Classic, Scholastic, and Humanistic Strains* (New York: Harper Torchbooks, 1961).

Kristeller, Paul Oskar. *Renaissance Thought II: Papers on Humanism and the Arts* (New York: Harper Torchbooks, 1965).

Lodge, Henry Cabot, gen. ed. *The History of Nations* (6th ed.; vol. 4: *Italy*; New York: P.F. Collier & Son, 1928).

Lucki, Emil. *History of the Renaissance* 5 vols. (Salt Lake City, Utah: University of Utah Press, 1963).

Luzia, A. and R. Renier. *Niccolo da Corregio* (Torino: Gionale Storica della Letterature Italiana, 1893).

Maulde la Clavière, Rene de. *The Women of the Renaissance*, trans. by G. H. Ely (New York: G.P. Putnam's Sons, 1901).

Martines, Lauro. *The Social World of the Florentine Humanists: 1390-1460* (London: Routledge and Kegan Paul, 1963).

Mattingly, Garrett. *Renaissance Diplomacy* (London: Butler and Tanner, 1963).

Morgan, Robin, ed. *Sisterhood is Powerful* (New York: Vintage Books, 1970).

Mozans, H.J. [J.A. Zahms]. *Women in Science* (New York: D. Appleton & Co., 1913).

Pelissier, Louis. *Les Armies de Ludovico Sforza* (Paris: Revue Historique, 1891).

Plumb, J. H. *The Italian Renaissance* (New York: Harper Torchbooks, 1961).

Power, Edward J. *Main Currents in the History of Education* (New York: McGraw-Hill, 1962).

Rice, Eugene F. *The Renaissance Idea of Wisdom* (Cambridge [Mass.] : Harvard University Press, 1958).

Seybolt, Robert F. *The* Manuale Scholarium: *An Original Account of Life in the Mediaeval University* (Cambridge [Mass.] : Harvard University Press, 1921).

Sismondi, J.C.L. *History of the Italian Republics in the Middle Ages*, ed. William Boulting (London: George Routledge and Sons, Ltd., 1895).

Spitz, Lewis W. *The Renaissance and Reformation Movements* 2 vols. (Chicago: Rand McNally and Co., 1972).

Symonds, John Addington. *The Renaissance* vol. 2: *The Revival of Learning* (London: Smith, Elder, and Co., 1897).

Torbriner, Marian Leona. *Vives'* Introduction to Wisdom: *A Renaissance Textbook* (New York: Columbia University Teachers Press, 1968).

Voigt, Georg. *Die Wiederbelung des Classichen Alterthums, oder das erste Jahrhundert des Humanismus* 2 vols. 2d ed. (Berlin: N.P., 1859).

Wise, John E. *The History of Education* (New York: Sheed and Ward, 1964).

Woodward, William H. *Studies in Education During the Age of the Renaissance: 1400-1600* (New York: Russell & Russell, 1965).

Woodward, William H. *Vittorino da Feltre and Other Humanist Educators* 2d ed. (New York: Columbia University Teachers College Press, 1963).

Magazines, Monographs, & Periodicals:

Carroll, Bernice A. "Mary Beard's *Women as Force in History:* A Critique", in *Women: An Issue*, ed. Lisa Baskins, Lee R. Edwards, and Mary Heath. (Boston: Little, Brown & Co., 1972).

Engstrand, Iris Wilson, "Student Life in the Mediaeval University," *History Journal* I (Spring, 1975): 53-62.

Gabriel, Astrik L. "The Ideal Master of the Mediaeval University," *The Catholic Historical Review* LX (April, 1974): 1-40.

Powers, Eileen. "The Position of Women," *The Legacy of the Middle Ages*, ed. C.G. Crump and E.F. Jacobs (New York: Oxford University Press, 1926).

Powicke, F.M. "Some Problems in the History of the Mediaeval University," *Transactions of the Royal Historical Society* 4th ser. XVII, p. 4.

Wright, Louis B. "Birth of a New Age," *The Renaissance*, ed. Melville Bell Grosvenor (Washington, D.C.: National Geographic Society, 1970).

INDEX

80